# CLEARING
# CRYSTAL
# CONSCIOUSNESS

Brotherhood of Life, Inc.
Albuquerque, New Mexico

Published in the United States of America by
Brotherhood of Life, Inc.
110 Dartmouth, SE
Albuquerque, NM 87106

ISBN 0-914732-17-X
First printing 1986
Fifth printing 1988

Acknowledgements:
The cover: © Daniel Valdes, Father Sky-Mother Earth
   Gallery, Santa Fe, NM

Received With Love
For The Healing Of The Earth

# CONTENTS

## PART II

# INTRODUCTION

This book has been written for the purpose of bringing enlightenment and knowledge to the practice of using natural quartz crystal for healing and meditation. Little is known today about the use of quartz crystal and consequently much mystery and illusion surrounds the crystal. Crystal energy, though unseen and often unfelt, is nevertheless a powerful energy which can create disturbance, damage and imbalance on many levels if it is not used cautiously by highly sensitive, skilled persons who are aware of the quality of energy with which they are dealing. Natural quartz crystal is more than a pretty rock. This mineral has the potential for containing and transforming energy beyond what contemporary man can conceive. It is important that crystals be used with consciousness and sensitivity to facilitate natural healing and growth rather than to create disharmony and imbalance. If one does not really know, then it is best not to attempt to use crystal. There are many well-intentioned people who think that they know how to use crystal or who have learned from others who think that they know. Working with crystal involves "knowing with"— and "knowing with" crystal is not the same as "knowing about" crystal.

"Knowing with" crystal is an active, dynamic, in-the-moment, now experience with unseen energy in constant motion. "Knowing about" crystal does not necessarily involve or include the ability of the healer to actually consciously experience the dynamic flow of crystal energy happening in the moment, or to have the ability to respond to the energy. This book is for those people who are interested in using quartz crystal consciously as a healing and meditation tool.

The revival and interest in the use of natural quartz crystal for healing is becoming increasingly widespread in the world but is subject to unintentional misuse. It is no accident that knowledge about the crystal remains limited to the physical dimension and that knowledge of how to use the crystal still remains a mystery for the most part. Information about the use of the crystal is coming into the world, but cautiously, to prevent the misuse of crystal energy. Every precaution is being taken to prevent misuse and few are the people to whom this information is given. This book will address these and other issues involved in using crystal. As there are many fine books available which deal extensively with the physical dimension of quartz crystal, this topic will not be discussed in this book.

*Christa Faye Burka*

# PART I

# CHAPTER I

# LIVING WITH CRYSTAL

This book has been brought forth into the world through the process of channeling as it is appropriate that this information be made available. The information within this book will be of benefit to many people who are involved in the use of natural quartz crystal or who contemplate future involvement with crystal.

Natural quartz crystal is becoming more and more popular. People from many walks of life are acquiring crystals for a variety of reasons and purposes. Some people are simply attracted by the sheer beauty of natural quartz crystal while others use quartz crystal for their personal meditation and prayer practices. Others are attempting to use quartz crystal for healing and energy work and some people are busy researching the crystal scientifically.

There are an abundance of theories, ideas and many illusions existing about the crystal as man attempts to comprehend it and its mysteries. With the exception of the known information about the physical qualities and function of quartz crystal, man has little understanding of the use of crystal energy. This book will help to clarify some of the difficulties involved in understanding and using quartz crystal.

Man has been living with quartz crystal since the beginning of time. Natural quartz crystal serves a vital function on the planet. Indeed, the continuous existence of the planet depends upon quartz crystal. Deep within the stratum of the earth's crust are located massive clusters of crystals which are strategically placed by nature. As with all dimensions of nature, these crystals are situated to create a perfect harmonious balance within the earth. The function of these crystals is to maintain the balance of the electro-magnetic field which surrounds the earth. The crystals balance the magnetic energy flowing between the north pole and the south pole thus maintaining the basic polarity of the planet. These large clusters also balance the electrical energy moving around the planet with the magnetic flow of energy. The pattern of energies surrounding the earth looks much like a web of many invisible intersecting lines forming an energy grid. The tension within this energy grid is maintained by these crystal clusters. Without the use of crystal, this energy grid would become unbalanced and the earth would lose its polarity creating much shifting and disturbance.

This same basic electro-magnetic field exists around everything, living and so-called non-living, that exists on the planet, right down to the cellular level and beyond that even to the atomic level. Each atom has this same invisible field and if contemporary science could witness the sub-atomic level, the same would be so here.

Indeed, this same basic field exists in systems at all levels: atomic, cellular, planetary, solar, galactic and universal. The essential balance and time-less movement within each system is maintained by an inner crystalline structure. This harmonious balance is perpetually maintained in nature without mankind needing to do anything nor to even understand this wondrous phenomenon. Aeon after aeon, civilization after civilization, moment-to-moment, man lives with crystal, unaware of the tremendous function of this brilliant, clear mineral.

Surrounding the human body is a similar invisible energy field arranged in a web-like fashion and forming an oval shape. This human energy field interfacets with the larger earth energy field. The human body has a north pole and a south pole, between which run the magnetic energies of the earth. This creates polarization within the body and also grounds man to the earth. Moving in a spiral fashion around and through the body is the universal life energy which is electrical in nature. These electrical and magnetic energies inter-connect and form an energy grid around the body. Similarly, each organ and each cell has its own balanced electro-magnetic field which inter-connects and inter-penetrates with the whole in complete harmonious balance. At the cellular level, this balance is maintained by the abundance of silica found within the human body which is the exact chemical composition of natural quartz crystal ($S_1O_2$). Silica is a major mineral within the body. This substance serves the same purpose in helping to maintain the energy fields within and around the body as the large crystals in the earth serve to maintain the energy field of the earth and solar system.

As long as balance is maintained within the energy field of the body, the body is in a state of health or wholeness. This happens naturally with many people without their awareness of the process. However, should the energy field become disturbed or imbalanced, the body may eventually become ill. Illness usually begins in the energy field of the individual and manifests in the physical body after a period of time. The condition of a person's energy field is then a predictor of potential disease in the body as well as an indicator of general body functioning. The appearance of being physically healthy is not evidence of health and may only suggest that disturbance and imbalance in the energy field has not yet manifested in the physical body. Health or wholeness is when all the energies within the body's energy field are in balance and are integrated.

Energy is not static but is in a constant state of flux and motion. Therefore, we are constantly moving between balance and imbalance, integration and disintegration, health and disease in our movement and evolution. Health is not a static condition nor is disease. We are not static creatures but are dynamic energy essences and our physical bodies process dynamic energy as does the crystal within nature. The crystal can help man gain greater awareness of himself as an energy being and with this awareness, the conscious balancing and integration of his energies or healing is possible.

The electro-magnetic energy fields of every form of life, whether human, animal, plant, or mineral, process dynamic energy through a form of crystal which creates states of balance in nature. Without this inter-action between energy and crystal, life as we know it on the physical level on this planet would not exist nor would the planet exist. Living with crystal involves a dynamic, vital process of nature with which each and every form of life is intimately involved.

# APPENDIX A

There are several suggested ways in which crystal energy can be used to enhance the quality of energy in a living space.

Amethyst quartz crystal is particularly beneficial in sleeping and meditation areas as the energy radiated from this crystal has a soothing effect upon the nervous system. This crystal contains the essence of the violet or purple ray in its purest form. Amethyst crystal emits a strong spiritual and healing energy.

Clear quartz crystal can be placed wherever the individual feels intuitively to place it. However, crystal should not be placed on or near electronic equipment or machinery as the crystal will absorb these energies which can interfere with its natural functioning. Wherever crystal is situated, it tends to enhance the qualities of energy manifesting in a certain area. Crystal kept in a bedroom will enhance the quality of the dreaming and sleeping states. Crystal kept in meditation areas enhances the meditation experience. As has been previously stated, crystals function naturally and will continue to do so without any active involvement of the individual. The crystals simply need to be present.

In order to facilitate the energy flow within a

crystal, it is best to keep it exposed and to point the tip of the crystal in a direction aligned with the magnetic energy flow of the earth. For example, point the base end of a crystal towards the north and the tip towards the south. You could also point the base of the crystal towards the east and the tip towards the west. This will facilitate the flow of energy within the crystal and thus affect the energy radiating from it.

The use of crystal in today's world is very much an individual matter and must be considered as such. For some people, it is not appropriate that they have crystal around them in any form. Other people are able to have much crystal energy near them. Some people can only have certain pieces or varieties of crystal near them for specific periods during their life. Each person is different and unique in his needs and these needs are continuously shifting and changing as individual energy shifts and changes, so that what is appropriate at one time is not appropriate at another time. Whatever your needs, nature or life provides for you. The particular crystals and stones which you are needing in your life will come to you. It is no accident that you have the crystals or stones you presently have. These stones and crystals can be passed along or will disappear when you no longer need them. If it is not appropriate for someone to have a crystal, it will disappear.

The stones and crystals which you have around you, at any particular time, are enhancing and supporting your growth and development and, in this sense, they act as a medicine. Native people around the world have long been aware of the power of crystal and stone to heal and to support growth. The ancient wisdom and knowledge of the use of the mineral kingdom is coming back into the world along with a strong revival of the use of the plant kingdom. Many of the natural healing tools available to humanity are being exhumed and revived as mankind approaches the end of the twentieth century. Natural healing is rapidly gaining support in the world today as man gains more awareness of himself and his wholeness as well as his connection with the whole. This current expansion of man's consciousness will manifest changes in how man perceives and utilizes the physical world and this will create change in his approach to healing himself. The future will see the merging of medical science with natural healing methods and this will reflect the deeper integration of mind and heart happening within man himself. There is much controversy and polarity today between medical science and natural healing methods but this simply reflects the conflict and confusion within man. Man considers himself to be scientifically well advanced at this time but it is evident that he still does not understand his basic inner nature. This inner imbalance creates imbalance in the outer world. The external reality reflects the inner reality and this is the reason why all healing, whether at the individual or global level, must begin with the individual. Each individual must re-establish his own inner balance and harmony as this is the very nature and essence of all healing.

# CHAPTER II

# WORKING WITH CRYSTAL

As has been discussed, crystals appear naturally within nature. This mineral is strategically placed and functions to balance, integrate and harmonize energy. The crystal performs this miraculous function without the involvement of man. Despite our lack of knowledge and awareness of crystal and how it functions, we are nonetheless deeply affected by it. This has been so for aeons, the natural balance just is.

Removing quartz crystal from its natural setting and using crystals in healing and energy work without knowing the potential effect of this mineral, is quite another matter. Now crystal has been used very successfully within electronic equipment such

13

as radios and computers to receive, store and trans-
mit information in the form of energy patterns.
These electronic devices work together with
electro-magnetic energy waves to receive and send
communications. This use of crystal serves man
without altering the natural balance of energy. Indeed, crystal has the capacity to serve mankind in
many ways yet undiscovered.

A limited amount of information about the appropriate use of crystal is being brought forth into
the world now. Knowledge of the use of crystal can
only come from spirit or from beyond the physical
dimension. The crystal functions beyond the current
experiential realm of man and beyond the scientific
investigations being undertaken at the present time.
Man is knowledgeable about and understands the
physical dimension of quartz crystal, however he is
presently unable to connect with, harness and uti-
lize the vital energy of the crystal. The dynamic energy of crystal functions beyond the intellectual
dimension of man and is indefinable. This is the
same dilemma man confronts when he attempts to
define the vital functioning of the human body. The
human body may be dissected, analyzed, and cate-
gorized but the soul and the spirit cannot be found.
This vital quality, which is our very aliveness, cannot be described within the framework of limited

definitions. Spirit is, by its very nature, indefinable. The energy of life, that pulsates in every body and everything, though unknowable scientifically, does nonetheless undeniably exist and is essential. To begin to "know" and "understand" vital life energy or spirit, man must make a quantum leap beyond the five senses into the world of the unknown and unknowable. So it is with crystals, for they function beyond the five senses, as well, beyond that which is known empirically by man. Crystal cannot be "known" via the scientific mental mode.

When you are working with crystal, you are working with the universal life energy of spirit. Therefore, it is most important that you are in touch with and connected to spirit, particularly your own. From this place, you can connect with all spirit, but that initial personal connection is fundamental to working with crystal. In this time, when so many people live in materialism and egoism, disintegrated within, it is rare to meet a person who actually experiences their connection to their spiritual dimension and who manifests these qualities in daily living. It is impossible for a person who does not have this inner spiritual connection to work consciously and effectively with others using crystal. Crystal functions as a bridge between the spiritual and the physical realms and the energy that crystal channels is both physical and spiritual in nature. The individual who is consciously connected to his spiritual energy will be sensitive to this same energy in the crystal and in others. Such a person will consciously and intuitively know more how to respond to the energy as it shifts and changes in himself and others.

When working with crystal with another person, two energy fields are involved, yours and the other person's. It is of vital importance that you know what is happening to the energy within the two fields and how the energies are affected by the crystal moment to moment. Your own energy is being affected if you are holding a crystal. If the other person is wearing or holding a crystal and you are not, you are, in effect, still using a crystal. You are being affected by the presence of the crystal as you are in that person's energy field. Energy fields interpenetrate and over-lap as physical bodies come closer together.

Working with crystals is a direct experience with energy as it moves moment to moment. There is no way to really "know about" working with crystal in the sense of developing standard techniques or methods which can be learned and applied to individuals. There are no standards when you work with energy. Each individual is unique and different and is changing energetically each second. It is impossible and even dangerous to work with crystal from a place of pure, learned technique. Crystal is currently being used predominantly in a technique-oriented way to manipulate the energy field of the human body. It is unwise to use crystal to affect another's energy without consciously knowing how to work with crystal energy. Knowing a technique does not mean that you are aware of energy or are able to respond to the energy appropriately. Without awareness and sensitivity to all of the energies present, the effect of working with crystal is similar to a surgeon operating in the dark. The crystal can function like a razor-sharp knife which penetrates the energy field of the body. This can create much disharmony and imbalance within the electromagnetic field and will also manifest in the physical body. You would not allow anyone but a skilled surgeon to penetrate your physical body with a knife. The same caution needs to be applied to your energy field as your bodies are not separate but inter-penetrate and integrate within the physical body. Without awareness, attunement and sensitivity, it is impossible to know where or how to manipulate a crystal within a person's energy field. Only in instances where consciousness and awareness of energy is involved should crystal ever be used to penetrate the energy field of another.

Each situation is different when you work with crystal. This is an individual matter. What works for one person may in fact be damaging and inappropriate for another. The use of crystals involves a tremendous response-ability. These minerals channel energies which can heal as well as damage with the same intensity and magnitude. To rely purely on technique or method does not allow for the spontaneous knowing of how to respond to the natural flow of energy. It is rather to confine oneself to a learned idea or belief of how to respond. This type of response may fit the technique but may not be in tune with what is really happening energetically with another in the moment.

One of the major roles of the crystal today is to help the individual bridge the gap and achieve integration between the physical and spiritual dimensions. A crystal is a tool and a gift from the universe to the person who is open and ready to receive it. Many people today are evolving consciously and to many of these people come crystals. Most people know intuitively which crystal feels right for them for the energy of the crystal resonates with the energy of the individual. These crystals become tools which can help the person's integration with his spiritual dimension as the crystal embodies within itself both the universal life energy of spirit as well as the magnetic earth energy. Through attunement with the crystal, the individual will begin to experience these energies within himself and the crystal. As this process continues, much awareness and many changes can begin to happen. Nothing needs to be done with the crystal, no technique needs to be used. Simply by attuning to the crystal, what needs to happen will begin to happen.

# APPENDIX B

It is possible for some people to work with crystal in the healing process. Such people have a deep sensitivity and intuitive ability to tune-in to the needs of the other person and will be able to act from this space of awareness rather than from a space of learned technique. In actual fact, the crystal will help the healer to gain deeper awareness and clarity of the needs of the other. It would be beneficial for people involved in healing work to have a crystal present in the work area. This crystal needs to resonate with the healer's energy and feel right for the healer. The crystal will help to keep the energy clear and moving towards awareness for both himself and the other person during sessions.

The healing process involves the healing of both the people involved simultaneously. In actuality, there is no healer or patient. There is only healing and this process goes on for both people. However, if one thinks he is "the healer" or is attached to being "the healer" at an ego level then a situation is created where the healer can only be the giver. He closes himself to the possibility of receiving from the other and thus thwarts his own healing. This situation can only be sustained for a short time before the healer is drained energetically. He has not allowed himself to be open to the natural flow of energy, the natural give and take needed to maintain balance. In such instances, the healer himself is responsible for disturbing his energy balance, not the client. Where there is a flow of energy, an exchange of energy between two people, both are energized. There is no healer nor client. You heal each other and it is important to understand this so that you may remain open to the gifts each has to offer. To be truly involved with the healing process is to be open to the other person. It is important to consciously honor this inter-play of energies to actualize the healing gifts of each person.

We are not negating the use of crystal in healing. Our purpose is to bring forth information on how crystal can be used to enhance the healing process today. It is important that we address ourselves to the present needs and world situation. How crystal have been used in the past is irrelevant at the present time. To attempt to duplicate past achievement is to expend energy trying to figure out and trying to adapt the past to meet the present needs and conditions. This is to miss the valuable use of crystal to man today to help him in the present world situation.

Crystal can be best utilized in the healing process

simply by being present. This is an indirect use of crystal but it is nonetheless highly effective in helping to clear energy and to bring clarity to situations. With recognition and awareness, healing begins to happen and dormant energies begin to move. Much can be done in this way of working as the link between consciousness and energy is direct. Raising consciousness raises energy. The flow of energy is stimulated, facilitating healing.

The basis and foundation for healing lies within the realm of consciousness. As man is ready to evolve into yet another level of consciousness, he commonly experiences disease. To heal himself, it is necessary to bring awareness and clarity to his situation. This will directly affect the movement of energy. There is a direct correspondence between consciousness and energy and this fact needs to be deeply understood by those in the healing professions. Healing is centered on this principle. Without awareness and clarity, you go on dealing with only the symptom, the manifestation of deeper imbalance. The symptom will continue to reappear until awareness is gained. The quality of awareness being discussed is not merely intellectual knowing but a deep inner knowing and recognition where you "know" what the significance of events mean for you personally. This level of knowing and awareness makes you free from that which makes you ill.

# CHAPTER III

# PLACEMENT OF CRYSTAL

As we have mentioned, crystals are intended to be utilized in the world today primarily for self-healing and self-growth. In this respect, the crystal becomes like an extension of the individual and serves as a bridge for the individual to connect with and experience unknown dimensions of the self. The crystal carries within it definite energies which resonate with the individual and can help the person to begin to become sensitive to these energies within himself. Now the crystal does not function overtly. It is necessary for the individual to attune to the subtle crystal energy. Heaven and earth meet within the crystal for the crystal channels the magnetic earth energies as well as the universal life energy of spirit. Through the process of attunement the

23

individual will begin to resonate with these energies and experience these energies as well as come into harmony and balance with these energies.

Balance is an integral and vital aspect of the healing process and the individual can create a balance of energies within a living space using several quartz crystals. It is to be noted that the individual does not need to do anything with the crystal but arrange them. Place crystals along a north wall or window with the points facing south. Place an equal proportion of crystal along the east wall with the points facing west. Consider the physical aspects such as size, weight and density of the crystal you are using as you want to create a balance of crystal energy along both the north and east wall. Clarity is not significant when selecting crystal for this use. Do not use double-terminated crystal for this purpose. Once the crystals are arranged the energy field within the room will balance naturally. Nothing needs to be done. You will notice the difference in the quality of the energy in the space. You will "feel good" in this harmonious, balanced energy and it will have a healing effect on you and help to balance your own energy. All living things whether mineral, plant, animal or human grow best in a balanced environment. Crystals can help you to create a balanced energy field in a living or working area.

There are numerous ways in which quartz crystal can be placed. However, each placement of crystal is unique and sets up a specific flow of energy which affects the energy field of the body in specific ways. These placements are known as energy grids and each grid serves a specific function. Energy grids are to be used with caution and much awareness as the energy flow of the grid can have a strong effect on the individual's energy and is not suitable for everyone. Much depends on the state of the individual's energy field which may or may not be in balance. While it is true that energy grids can create a state of balance, it is important to know which grid to use with which person. Energy grids have a definite value in the healing process but their use is best determined by energy-sensitive and aware individuals.

Regardless of how or where crystal is placed, whether on the body, in a bedroom, around a room or in a grid formation, crystal functions naturally through the process of resonance. To become sensitive to this process, one must attune to the crystal energy. Attunement is to come into at-one-ment with the crystal energy. Resonance is the natural process of crystal and the most effective way in which crystal can be used by the individual. To focus on techniques in the use of crystal is to miss the real function and value of quartz crystal in the world today.

# APPENDIX C

The universe is expansive and at the same time it is contained within the smallest particle. The very structure of the universe is reflected in the structure of the atom and within the cells which come together to form the human body. Each form in existence is a composite of a unique and specific arrangement of atoms and cells which combine to create a specific form to perform a specific function within the whole. The atom contains energy that is manifesting on the physical level to create form. Beyond the atom, at the sub-atomic level, there is nothingness, no form, only energy. This is often referred to as the void and is the space many people experience during deep meditation. However, the void is not void. Though it is void of form, it is alive and pulsating with energy. To experience the void is to experience the source or nothingness from which all form comes.

The other side of form is formlessness but this is not deadness. The formless is energy alive and vibrating at high frequencies beyond the capacity of the human physical sense organs to detect. The formless is alive and exists though you cannot see it with your physical eyes. The sub-atomic level vibrates with such high frequency that form cannot manifest as on the physical level where vibrations are much slower.

Within the formless lies the form and within the form lies the formless. Within the form of your physical bodies lies the formlessness of your subtle energy bodies. These energy bodies interpenetrate each other and connect within the physical body. The sub-atomic level of your beingness is both within and without the atomic or physical level. The subtle energy bodies are included within the physical body. You are not separate bodies. You do not in fact have separate bodies though you talk about your bodies as being separate or as being at different levels. In actual fact, you are one body, a manifestation and integration of different energies merging into a whole within the physical body.

The higher the vibration, at the sub-atomic level, the finer the energy of the subtle energy bodies. The finer the energy the closer to spirit you come while the denser the energy, the closer to the physical you come. If you want to connect with your spiritual or formless dimension you must move through the physical dimension or form as the formless is contained within the form. There is an intimate connectedness between all of your dimensions or subtle bodies which exists within the very atoms that form your cells. This cellular bonding of energies begins at conception and completes at birth. The bonding continues until it is terminated at death when you withdraw your energy and detach from the physical dimension.

The basis for all form is spirit. When form is penetrated, as has been done through quantum physics research, beyond the atomic level, you arrive at the energy of spirit. Spirit is the essence of all and is that from which all emerges and returns. Spirit is not something external to man. It is his source and is that which beats his heart and sees his eyes and hears his ears. The energy of spirit vibrates within every cell of your bodies.

It is impossible to become spiritual without first becoming physical. To connect with the inner master, with your spirit, is to return to the root and source of the physical body. Physicality is not against God. Physicality is an expression of God.

# CHAPTER IV

# GENERATING OF
# CRYSTAL

To fully understand this discussion, it is important that man understands the delicate balance which exists in nature as well as the fundamental laws of energy as crystals deal with energy and follow the laws of energy. From this place man can see and appreciate that he is a part of nature, that he affects the whole of nature and is affected by the whole of nature. He exists within the whole, not separately, as he might tend to think.

Every action or thought expressed by man puts out an energy pattern in the universe which creates an effect in the universe. Many people think that they are victims of fate, of what happens to befall them in life, not realizing that they simply get back what they put out into the universe. The universe is impartial, non-judgemental and simply responds with the same energy it receives from you. In this way, you create your own reality and your experience of life is uniquely your experience. For every person on this planet, there is a different reality. Your experiences of life are uniquely your own and may in fact not even correspond to what truly is. However, your experiences create your reality as your energy is altered by your experience and awareness and you express this energy in some form into the universe. The quality of energy you express and resonate with attracts a response of the same quality. Energy simply moves in response to a stimulus and altering the quality of energy expressed immediately alters the response.

Another fundamental law of energy is that energy is constantly in a state of motion and change. Energy is more like water than any other element. It flows and shifts and changes form as can be seen when water changes form from solid to liquid to gas. The energy is transmuted and changed in each instance. Energy is transmuting continuously both within you and the universe. You are in a constant state of motion and change, however imperceptible this process is to your physical senses.

Crystals channel energy in a state of natural balance and continual motion. Crystals, by their very nature, are self-generating. They generate the appropriate amount of energy to maintain a natural balance between the universal life energy and the magnetic energy flowing through them. Crystals magnify or amplify the energy of their environments. Like the universe, they are impartial and simply amplify energy. If "negative" energy is happening, this will be amplified. If "positive energy" is happening, this will be amplified. This amplification of energy can help the individual who is involved in self-healing to become aware of the different qualities of energy within himself and his environment. Through attunement, the individual will begin to resonate with the flow of energy and with this awareness comes the possibility of change, transmutation and healing.

Becoming energy sensitive and aware is a gradual process, a relaxation and a surrender. It involves a letting-go of doing and a focusing of your attention inwards. This process may involve simply sitting quietly or meditating while holding a crystal in your hand. Each person will discover their own unique way and time to tune-in to themselves.

While holding a crystal, begin to become more and more aware of the flow of your energy as you feel and experience the movement in and around your body. Try placing the crystal directly on areas where the energy feels low until you feel the area pulsate again. Keep the crystal pointing head-toe when you do this. Trust your intuition about your energy and be guided by your innate feelings.

When you experience your energy, you experience your aliveness and vitality and you can trust your aliveness and begin to allow your energy to move you in harmony with what feels right for you rather than you imposing many "shoulds" on your energy, thereby controlling the spontaneous flow of your energy. However, to respond naturally to energy involves becoming energy aware as well as conscious in the expression of energy. Responding to energy naturally is not suggesting that people be allowed irresponsible freedom of expression that may harm themselves or others. Responding to energy involves awareness and choice. It is the ability of the individual to respond appropriately to the energy in the moment. This is the true significance of the word "responsibility" for it involves the integrity and awareness of the individual in his response to life. Being responsible for your life does not mean you are guilty for your life as is so often inferred. This is in fact using the word "responsible", irresponsibly.

At each moment you have choice and it is precisely in these moments that you can begin, step-

by-step, to change your life and alter deeply conditioned patterns of action and reaction. When your
energy becomes heart-directed rather than mind-
directed or emotionally-directed, you will respond
with right action which is in harmony with the
whole. When your heart is into doing something,
all of your energy becomes available to you and
you become alive in your expression. Doing something because you think you should, when your
heart does not want to, creates resistance in the
heart. This resistance blocks the full flow and expression of your aliveness. It is important to focus
on and consider what your heart wants so that you
may come in touch with your soul needs rather
than your neurotic needs.

Nature has created, within each crystal, the appropriate amount of energy for each crystal. The
natural energy within each crystal is balanced and
sufficient for use in the world today. Any alteration
of a crystal's energy or vibration by mechanical
means creates a disturbance in the natural energy
balance. This alters the healing potential of the
crystal and alters the quality of healing that can occur. A highly-charged crystal does not facilitate
healing. Healing is, in itself, a process of coming
into natural balance.

Within the universe, there is a source of crystal

energy. This is not a physical place but rather an energy place. From this source, energy manifests on the earth in the form of crystal. The energy generating within each crystal is exactly right. All is perfect in nature.

# APPENDIX D

The energy channeling through the crystal is sacred energy. It is the life energy of the universe, the pulse of the universe which gives life to everything in the universe. In this sense, the energy is sacred for nothing would exist without this energy. It fills our bodies at birth and retreats from our bodies at death. There is a constant ebb and flow of this energy. It has its own rhythm and its tides are beyond the control of man. This ocean of energy penetrates all. The flow of life energy simply is whether you are talking at a universal or individual level. As man becomes more in touch with his own natural energy flow, he begins to fall into synchronization with the universal flow of energy. When this happens, life works. Events connect and flow together without interruption or disturbance. There is no resistance to the natural flow of energy. When life is filled with obstacles and disruptions, it is important to determine if you are in any way controlling, disrupting, or limiting the natural flow of your own energy. If this is happening, you are not in harmony with the universe. There needs to be a total surrender to the natural flow of energy. Only then can you begin to resonate and move with the universal ocean of energy. This process involves the presence, the alive awareness and sensitivity of the individual to his energy as well as the individual's ability to respond to his energy appropriately. It is only when the individual is able to respond to his own energy needs, in the moment, that he becomes able to respond to and to meet the energy needs of others. You cannot give to others what you do not give to yourselves or do not already possess within yourselves. You cannot love unconditionally until you first love yourself unconditionally and actually experience a deep acceptance and love for yourself exactly as you are. The person who is able to respond to his own energy will be able to respond to another's energy sensitively and harmoniously. This is an important and significant quality for people who are actually involved in using crystals in healing. If this quality or ability is lacking in the healer, he will be equally limited in his ability to respond to and meet another's energy needs.

Man must first learn to honor and respect the natural flow of his own energy and the natural balance of energy within the universe before he is able to work with and use the sacred energy of the crystal. He must learn to live in harmony with universal life energy rather than as a manipulator and master of energy. The ability to simply allow the flow and balance of energy to happen naturally is fundamental and essential to connecting with and using the sacred crystal energy. To connect with the universal life energy within crystal you must connect with the universal life energy in you. The real power or energy of crystal comes from spirit. Crystals are empowered and generated with energy patterns from spirit which are imprinted within the crystal.

Previously, the sacred crystal energy was abused and man lost his connection to the source of this energy in the universe. Now this energy source is again becoming available to the world but in a way which will teach man how to use crystal together with basic principles involved in using crystal. This book is an initial step in this process. Until this information is understood and accepted, knowledge of the generating of crystal energy will remain limited.

# CHAPTER V

# STORING CRYSTAL

During a person's life-time, many different crystals and stones will come to them at different times. These minerals are all given to you for a specific purpose though you may or may not be conscious of it. Many minerals can come in and out of a person's life. Products of the mineral world are helpers or tools and come to you via mysterious ways and can often leave just as mysteriously.

There are many ways in which crystal can be used to enhance a person's life. Each individual has his own unique need for crystal. Crystal functions in specific ways for the individual and this function, in part, determines where to keep the crystal. In general, the crystal just needs to be available for whatever function it is to serve. Crystal does not need to be kept on the body; it may be kept on a table or counter. From this place, crystal can perform its function effectively yet unobtrusively. The more energy sensitive you become, the more you will feel the crystal energetically. The crystal radiates a continuous flow of energy which interacts with the human energy field. This is so with all products of the mineral world. Each mineral has its own unique vibration just as the human body has. The vibrations of minerals interact and resonate with the body's vibration creating a healing affect. Now this process goes on continuously in the world whether or not you are conscious of it or even accept it. The universe continues to function according to the timeless laws of nature. You do not need to do anything with a crystal, except to have it present where you want it and it will function as nature intended. Trust in the wisdom of nature and the crystal will become a valuable tool for your growth and healing.

Trust your intuition about where to keep crystals. As crystals absorb energy, it is best not to keep them in areas where there is an intense vibration such as on top of electrical equipment or machinery. Crystals which are specifically for supporting a person in his work need to be in the work area. The dream is, for many people, an important vehicle for growth and integration. Dream crystals come to some people to help them gain clarity and awareness through the dream. These crystals need to be kept uncovered by the bedside. Some people are fortunate to receive a crystal which so closely matches and resonates with their own energy that the crystal is like an extension of the person's energy. Such a crystal vibrates with the same frequency as the individual and seems to manifest the essence of the person's energy within it. These crystals have much personal significance and are life crystals capable of serving the individual for life. They are tremendous tools for self-growth and self-healing and are best kept in a living or sleeping space. The individual will feel a strong, magnetic-like attraction to such a crystal.

When crystals are being transported, it is best to keep them in a soft pouch to protect them from physical damage as well as altering the quality of energy simply from exposure to the many vibrations in your environment. This will help to keep the crystal clear of extraneous energy.

As crystals constantly channel energy, they are essentially self-clearing and self-cleansing. There is no need for elaborate cleansing techniques, unless this makes you feel better, but it is not necessary for the crystal. To stimulate the flow of energy and thus the cleansing and clearing of the energies of crystal, simply put the crystal in the direct sunlight for one to two hours and this will enliven the energy. You could do this whenever you feel that it is necessary.

While it is true that the potential use of the crystal is beyond man's present capacity to understand, the crystal does not have any mystical power. The crystal simply follows the laws of energy and nature in its functioning. It is man who has the power to choose how to use the energy of the crystal.

# APPENDIX E

In terms of storing crystal for longer periods of time, it is best to insure that the crystal is protected from a lot of extraneous energy in the environment. Pack crystal in dense fabrics or materials and place them in stable containers which can be closed. It is beneficial to keep these containers at ground level and if at all possible below ground level. This will help to neutralize the energy of the crystal as the earth is a most potent transformer of energy. Following long periods of storage, bury the crystals directly in the earth for one week with no wrapping on the crystal. Then rinse the crystal and bring it out into the direct sunlight for a couple of hours to enliven the energies. The crystal will become virgin again in its pureness of energy.

Crystals which are being stored for a short time can be buried directly in the earth. This is an opportunity to neutralize and cleanse the crystal as well as to protect it. Expose the crystal to sunlight to rejuvenate the energy flow afterwards. With crystal which you keep with you or wear, it is suggested that you periodically allow time for this neutralization process.

Crystals do not like to be kept in high noise areas nor do they like synthetic fabrics as these fabrics do not permit the natural flow of energy. In the care of crystal, let naturalness be your criteria for the crystal is natural and resonates best with nature.

# CHAPTER VI

# PAIN AND CRYSTAL

Pain is created in areas of the physical body, where energy has become contracted or limited in its natural tendency to flow throughout the body. This situation can be created by such things as trauma, disease, stress, and many other factors which affect the lives of human beings. The onset of physical pain can often be foreseen in the aura of people where psychological and emotional imbalance first occurs. If these energies are not cleared and harmonized through the appropriate means, the disharmony created by psychological and/or emotional distress will manifest in the physical body as disease. Energy expresses itself one way or another. If energy is not expressed outwardly it expresses inwardly in the form of disease in the body.

Disease is the body's way to clear itself of re-pressed, stuck energy. Pain is a signal. It is like an alarm clock. It is nature's way of telling you that something is wrong, to stop and listen to the message of the pain, to discover the disharmony within the bodymind which is creating the disease.

Disease is a symptom of a disturbance at a much deeper level. Most diseases which man manifests during his life-time fall into this range. Therefore, in order to cure disease, it is usually necessary to go deep within the psychological and emotional dimensions and heal these levels also. Often, this is the root cause of disease in the physical body. The pain which results from the disturbance is the body screaming for your attention. In this sense, pain is a gift of nature to help show you that you are out of harmony and balance and is nature's signal to you to focus your attention on the real issues. However, all too often, people see pain as being against them and as something that they need to get rid of as quickly as possible so they take a pill which dulls and masks the pain and which creates the illusion that the disease is controlled or cured. People need to see and understand the basic nature of pain and to know that pain is not against them. Only then will man be able to begin to focus within and truly begin to heal himself.

Many people have been known to cure themselves of disease, in a short time, by moving deeply inside themselves in an isolated soul search. Such people are often able to identify the roots of their disease and in this recognition and acceptance, they change the energy pattern which created the disease, releasing and clearing the energy. Within these people is a deep acceptance and recognition of their responsibility in the creation of disease and disharmony. They do not see themselves as victims and accept responsibility for changing the dis-ease into ease.

The individual who thinks or feels like a victim of pain and disease is at a distinct disadvantage in initiating and maintaining the self-healing process for the victim is one who is always looking outside himself for causes and cures. Little does he know or want to know of his responsibility in the creation of his disease. The word responsibility is used here to indicate a person's response-ability or ability to respond appropriately to life. Most people are unable to respond to their life situations in ways which are consistently nurturing and wholesome. You do the best you can in the moment and respond to life with the resources and awareness you have within and there is no blame. It is your unnourishing, habitual, conditioned patterns of response to life which are needing to be released with acceptance, awareness, clarity and love as these patterns create the disharmony and disease.

To begin to alter your response patterns, it is necessary to see and accept that you have choice. This, in itself, is an important recognition for many people and is the initial step to creating self-change. Choice is your only freedom. Through choice, you can begin to alter old patterns of response and try on new responses which are more nourishing and which are in harmony with your present needs. In this way, you become more available in the present and begin to stop recreating the past because you are choosing to change the energy patterns now. Energy patterns can only be altered in the present because energy is only alive now. Energy is a now phenomenon. In altering conditioned response patterns, you alter energy and break up bound up energy of the past which is creating present disharmony and disease. Energy from the past can only be transmuted and cleared in the present. Therefore, it is important to bring the past into the present to clear the energy. In this way, you free yourselves from the past and can consciously begin to create your life.

In dealing with pain, a surrender is required, a surrender to the pain, rather than a struggling to control the pain. Surrender is not resignation. Resignation is a giving up, a closing and a contracting. Surrender is an opening, an expansion into the pain, an acceptance and a willingness to see and to hear the inner message. The path to wholeness involves embracing pain rather than avoiding pain or masking pain. While many would prefer to ignore this statement, it is nonetheless the step mankind must take to regain harmony and balance within himself and the world.

With clarity and awareness man will be able to change his patterns of relating. Clarity is the essence of crystal. Indeed, the crystal represents the growth from unconsciousness to consciousness, simply in its physical nature. The growth of the crystal, to a perfect point, reflects the growth towards awareness and enlightenment beyond which the point of the crystal disappears into nothingness just as man disappears into nothingness when he clears, transmutes, and integrates his energy within a perfect point, he merges with the source.

As clarity is the essence of the crystal, the presence of crystal will function to bring clarity to pain regardless of whether the pain is physical, mental or emotional. The crystal is the tool available for man to use as he begins the transition into the New Age. This valuable mineral is a gift from nature given to man to use. However, it is vital that this gift not be misused and that it be used as it is intended in the evolution of man and the earth. Crystal is for the specific use of self-healing and self-growth. No other use of crystal is appropriate now. Attempting to recreate ancient methods of use of crystal energy will meet with limited success at this time. It is important that man honor and use this gift for his self-healing rather than to enhance his ego or to increase his power. Crystal is a natural healing tool which can help man as he begins to embrace his pain and direct the focus of his energy within to heal himself. You can receive much guidance and support from others but ultimately, you are your own healer. Nobody can heal you but you.

# APPENDIX F

It is important to understand that nothing outside of yourself can heal you. You are the only person who can do this. As long as you look outside of yourself for someone or something to heal you, you will miss the opportunity to heal the deep inner source of disease.

Quartz crystal has tremendous potential for use in man's growth in awareness as crystal energy resonates with all of the energies of the body including the mental body. Through resonance and attunement energies can become consciously known and experienced. The body is itself like a liquid crystal which channels much energy. The growth in consciousness and awareness involves the clearing of energies at all levels of your beingness: physical, mental and emotional. As these energies become clearer and clearer, locked-in energy is released thus releasing pain. Your total energy system becomes more and more pure in its nature. You become like a clear crystal. Your energies clear, transmute and merge into one harmonious energy . As your energy becomes clear, you become a pure channel for universal life energy. You become your own crystal as you integrate and connect directly with your spiritual dimension. There is no longer any separation between the spiritual and the physical.

The process of healing involves the integration of all the disintegrated or fragmented parts of yourselves through the acceptance of all of your energies and the allowing of the natural clear expression of these energies. Energy transmutes itself naturally through clear, complete expression. You do not need to consciously manipulate or control energy in any way to change or transmute energy. You only need to express energy. Energy is meant to be expressed and the existence of most pain in the body is the unexpressed, locked-in emotional energy of many years. Feelings and emotions are the natural expression and memory of the soul. It is unnatural to deny, repress, control or manipulate feelings. To deny feelings is to alienate your soul and create disintegration within you. This is an invitation to disease.

# CHAPTER VII

# THE CHAKRAS AND CRYSTAL

The chakras deal with the movement and the distribution of universal life energy throughout the body. The human body functions, like a crystal, to channel this energy through the chakra system and to distribute this energy within the body. As long as the body is clear and free from tension, this energy flows unimpeded with its own momentum. However, when natural expression is blocked, energy contracts and ceases to express or radiate. The energy of the chakras can become impure when the energy system is not expressing or distributing itself in a state of balance.

Perhaps one of the most significant uses of crystal can be to help to clear and to balance the energy of the chakra system. To clear and to balance the energy of the chakra system, place the base of a crystal on the physical body at the site of the chakra and point the tip away from the body. Hold the crystal lightly with both hands and keep it in place for approximately 15 minutes. It is important to use a crystal that resonates with your body energy. This clearing and/or balancing of the chakra system can be done as part of an individual's meditation or relaxation period, as the person feels to do. Nothing else needs to be done. You will begin to experience the energy balancing and the chakra's radiating energy fully and openly. You do not need to use affirmations, visualizations or imaging techniques. Visualization does not make the crystal function any better. The crystal functions scientifically and naturally and it will go on functioning as such despite whatever mystique you create around it. Rather than actively engaging the mind at such times, it would be far more beneficial to relax the mind and to allow yourself to attune to the movement of energy happening in the body and in the crystal.

Creation has given man a special tool with which to help him move beyond a mind-focus into an energy-focus. As crystal magnifies energy, man can come to experience another dimension of himself and can begin to bring balance and harmony to his energies. His energies can then become consciously directed rather than his energies unconsciously controlling him.

Consciousness and energy are mutually affected. What happens in one dimension affects the other. As man becomes more in touch with his own consciousness, his energy will begin to change and transmute along with his consciousness. The crystal is the tool given to man to help him in his growth and evolvement into the New Age. The New Age is the age of integration. It is the time in the evolution of man when all of his energies will become balanced and integrated. The New Age is an inner space as well as an outer space. It is represented by the integration and balance of the trinity of energies of bodymind, soul and spirit.

# CHAPTER VIII

# STORING ENERGY IN THE CRYSTAL

Working with crystal, as has been brought forth in this book, involves working with yourself first to heal yourself. When you have come to inner balance and integration, then you will know how to use crystals. This knowing will be a deep inner recognition and revelation rather than a learned intellectual understanding. You will know and appreciate the magnificence of crystal for it reflects the magnificence of you and your essence.

When man is balanced within his heart, he will be given guidance from spirit on how to store and use the powerful crystal energy to meet his daily needs. Information will come through from spirit about crystals as is appropriate for man to know. This knowledge is and will be important and signifi-

cant for man at the time it is received. Working
with the sacred crystal energy requires guidance
from spirit as you are dealing with energy which
has the power to heal as well as destroy. Few are
the people to whom this information will be given.
The truth and authenticity of this information will
be recognized and known within the heart of the
individual reader.

As information about the use of crystals is now
becoming available to the world, it is important
that man understand the deeper principles being
presented here so that misuse of crystal energy does
not inadvertantly occur. These deeper foundational
principles must be understood within the heart as
well as the mind. Though some would dispute
these principles, they nonetheless form the basis for
all work with crystal and the understanding of these
principles is the first step towards working with
crystal.

# CHAPTER IX

# CREATING THE
# SPIRITUAL CONNECTION
# THROUGH CRYSTAL

We have talked about resonance and attunement in relationship to the function or use of crystal. To this we would like to add that attunement involves a process of turning inward, of de-focusing on the external world and the out-flow of energy, and to simply focusing on the inner world and the movement of your energy in the present moment.

There are many techniques available to help develop this process and each person will find their own unique technique that works best for them. The most significant factor is that the technique facilitates the inner focusing of attention. It is also important that the technique be recognized for what it is, a technique that you will be able to let-go of eventually to allow the spontaneous movement of natural process. The wide variety of relaxation, awareness, and meditation techniques, currently being practiced, serve a vast number of people with different needs. Through these techniques, your attention is focused more within the body and its energy rather than on the mind and its contents. There is a de-emphasis on the mind as attention begins to shift and at the same time there is a corresponding shift in energy as energy always flows where attention flows. This movement or shift of attention and energy away from the mind is essential to experiencing the here and now. The present moment can never be experienced directly through the mind or thought. Mind functions in the past or future. The present dimension is only truly experienced when you can slip out of your thoughts and just be here, relaxed into the moment. This process requires actual practice as the mind has become the habitual focal point of energy, particularly in the western world. Gradually, the mind will cease its chatter and you will experience yourself more aware of the moment, more in-tune with the flow of your energy and your environment and you will experience other ways of knowing that do not directly involve the mind. An intuitiveness and deep inner knowing will begin to surface along with many other experiences which may reveal dimensions of yourself that you have hitherto not known.

Your spiritual dimension can only be experienced in the present moment. God is experienced only in the present moment and when you come to live in the moment with awareness, you come to know God. God is not removed from you, He is hiding in the eternal moment and you only need to be present to begin to know this.

Each person needs to trust their own process and their inner knowing. Often experiences of knowingness and presence can happen spontaneously and become more and more frequent as your energy shifts away from the mind. Thinking that you are in the moment is not the same as being in the moment. If you think you are in the moment, you are not in the moment, you are in your mind. This is tricky and needs to be experienced to know the difference. Being in the moment is a surrender of mind activity, a pure presence of your beingness and awareness.

There are some for whom this process occurs naturally without effort or practice. Such people seem ageless, vital and alive despite their physical age. There is a brilliant, sparkling clarity within their eyes. These people do not live in time. They live now, no past, no future, only now. They sit on the edge of time and watch the parade of time pass by them. They are simply present.

Becoming present is the gateway to your spiritual dimension, to knowing your oneness with all and your wholeness as well as to integrating your spiritual and physical dimensions. To experience your wholeness is to experience the balance and integration of the trinity of your energies and through this, you will know your essence.

The movement just discussed is fundamental to creating a spiritual connection and can indeed be done without the use of crystal. The function of crystal is to enhance the process by helping to increase energy awareness. Crystal is a bridge between the physical and the spiritual dimensions. As crystal magnifies and clarifies energy, it can help the individual experience his energy with greater sensitivity and awareness through the attunement process. Crystal can then help to de-focus from the mind and bring attention to the energy body and in this way the individual can become more consciously present, in the moment, as energy only happens now.

There is much controversy in the world today surrounding the issue of spirituality. Attempting to define spirit or spirituality is impossible and is erroneous right from the start as definitions come from the mind, from words, the product of the mind. At best these words can only describe limited aspects of spirit but they cannot capture the essence of spirit. It is analogous to attempting to create bricks with a substance that is like water. Words tend to confine when they are used to define. Spirit can only be experienced and known directly in the present moment. As you come to experience the natural flow of your aliveness and vitality, moment-to-moment, you will begin to experience God or spirit in each moment and you will discover that you have always been where you have wanted to be but may not have consciously known it.

# APPENDIX G

It is important that man understands and appreciates that the source of crystal energy and power is spirit. The energy of quartz crystal has been evolving over millions of years through a process of refining, clarifying and purifying. The pureness of this mineral resonates with the purest of energy and attracts and channels this energy through it.

A solid piece of crystal contains within it a myriad of atoms all vibrating at a specific frequency. Each atom carries an electrical charge and it is within this charge that energy patterns can be received, stored and transmitted. The crystal functions similarly to the human brain. Both are receivers of energy in the form of electrical impulses from the vast universe. Neither has the capacity or ability to function independently but rather absorbs or collects and amplifies energy patterns from the universe through resonance. The energy patterns or information received by the brain depend mainly on how open you are to the unknown. You only receive what you are willing to know about. Thus, your knowledge is limited only by your willingness to open to the new or the unknown. You pick up and receive exactly what you want to receive.

Unlike the human brain, which censors information, the crystal is simply open to receive energy from the universe. The crystal acts as a conduit of this energy, transforming, magnifying and radiating energy out into the world.

Clear quartz crystal contains the full spectrum of the energy of the seven rays. Every color and every vibration related to these rays, which pertain specifically to the earth plane, is contained within clear quartz crystal. Herein lies the secret to the potential of quartz crystal to balance energy, to create awareness and to heal at all levels. Each of the seven rays directly corresponds to the seven major energy centers or chakras of the body. As the clear crystal contains each of the seven rays, this crystal can act on all of the chakras to stimulate and balance the total energy system simultaneously. When energy is balanced a state of clarity and awareness naturally emerges.

Quartz crystal also receives and transmits the magnetic earth energies which ground the universal life energy of spirit within the crystal. The energy of spirit and physical energy become integrated and naturally balanced within the crystal. The spiritual energy of the crystal is firmly rooted in the physical energy of the crystal and this grounding is essential to and is the foundation for crystal growth.

Likewise with man, the firm rooting and integration of his spiritual energy with his physical energy forms the essential foundation upon which growth can flourish.

When the spiritual and the physical dimensions become bridged and separation no longer exists, man becomes a pure, clear, channel for universal life energy. In effect, he becomes his own crystal and would not need to use the external crystal. Such a person would be able to work with crystal with a deep integrity as this person would be guided by his heart in its use. Individuals who have cleared and transmuted their own energy system must be centered and focused in their heart. Knowing this, they can do no wrong and could work safely with crystal if they choose.

# CHAPTER X

# OPENING BEYOND BELIEF

There is much emphasis today within the various growth groups on belief structures and on how these beliefs create your reality. Now this is a significant and important fact to be understood. What you believe is so. In other words, what you think is true is what you experience as true. It is as if the universe fulfills your beliefs and gives to you that which you expect. Your deep-seated belief structure forms the foundation for your experience and therefore if you want to change your experience, you need to probe deeply into this structure carefully examining each belief. It is much the same as renovating the foundation of a house, discarding irrelevant, narrow, limiting beliefs and maintaining those beliefs which are supportive and life-promoting. This is a valuable process for people to become involved with during their life-time as this is a clearing and cleansing of the mental body. There are many techniques available to work with this clearing process such as visualization, affirmations, imaging and guided fantasy. These techniques are very effective at evolving the mental body and opening the mind to new possibilities. If you cannot imagine something happening first in your mind, it will not happen. All things manifest first in the mind as a thought and secondly, in the physical dimension. This is a fundamental law of manifestation. It is very important that this law or principle be honored and acknowledged as a significant and potent factor affecting one's total growth process. However, it is equally important to see that this is only one dimension or area of your totality which needs clearing and healing.

While it is true that the condition of the mental body affects your experiences as well as other levels of your being, to focus only on changing the mental body is to ignore the relevance and vital function of the other dimensions within your total beingness. It is equally important to heal and evolve the emotional body simultaneously to create inner connection, integration and balance. While there is much credibility and good coming out of the many mind-oriented healing processes today, it is vital that man not limit his growth in this dimension only by believing that if he changes his mind, he will change all. In other words, this belief can become yet another limitation to man in his growth towards integration and balance. Man is more than a mind. All dimensions of man need to be healed and brought into harmony.

It is impossible to clear and heal the emotional body through the mind. The emotional body must be approached through the heart not the mind. The emotional body feels while the mental body thinks and these are two different modes of expression which cannot be inter-changed. The language of the heart is emotion which wants to express naturally. Emotions are the movement and expression of the energy of the emotional body and this energy is constantly changing. It is important that you clear, integrate and evolve this level of your being-ness by dealing directly with these energies, in the present. The heart does not understand words, it cannot reason so it cannot be healed only through the use of words or thought. The heart cries and utters a message beyond the scope of words and in this way the emotional body is cleansed, cleared and healed. It is important to accept and express the energy of the emotional body directly in order

to create balance. To ignore, deny or judge any
emotion or energy of the emotional body is to miss
a crucial connection and source of energy necessary to your healing and integration. Disconnecting
from your emotions or your feeling self by attempting to control this dimension with the mind is to
disconnect from your aliveness and your vitality. As
you deaden your feelings, you lose your aliveness
as well as your spontaneity and you become mono-
tone. Emotional energy will and does find expression either directly or indirectly. This energy does
express in one way or another. You are alive, feeling organisms responding to a life that is constantly
changing moment-to-moment. It is unrealistic to
expect that you can move through life with a con-
sistent controlled emotional response. To respond
to life in such a manner, is to be frozen or controlled by a rigid belief of how one should be rather
than to allow a spontaneous response to life. This is
in no way suggesting that you allow your feelings or
emotions to control your response or action in life.
The emotional level is again, only one level of our
beingness, just as the mind is only one dimension.
The appropriate response or right action to life
comes when the feeling self and the thinking self
can come together. When there is agreement and
harmony between these two dimensions, then you
automatically move into the heart and right action

will follow. You can trust this for the heart is the meeting place or merging site of these energies. The fire of the emotional body meets and merges with the light of the mental body within the heart and right action must follow. Without the harmonious merging of these energies, you respond to life predominantly from an emotional basis or a mental basis, both of which are unbalanced. Balance occurs when the emotional and mental bodies integrate and merge.

To connect with your spiritual dimension or higher self, it is necessary to go through the heart. The spiritual dimension can never be reached through the mind but must be contacted through the merging of the emotional and the mental body within the heart. It is, therefore, essential to heal both these dimensions to facilitate the spiritual integration. This cannot be accomplished purely through the mind nor purely through the emotions. The link between the mental and emotional bodies is strong and it needs to be recognized that these dimensions interact continuously and to create balance within and between these dimensions is essential to healing the whole person and to facilitating the connection to the spiritual dimension.

Being spiritual does not mean to be unfeeling or controlled. Being spiritual is being whole and wholeness happens through acceptance, integration and balance. Wholeness is the balancing of the trinity of your energies of bodymind, soul and spirit.

Through the acceptance and integration of your feeling self with your thinking self, you can bring awareness to your actions and you can know that you have a choice in how you respond to life. This knowing can make you free. You do not need to be controlled by emotions but can make conscious choices to respond differently. In this way, you become response-able and this gives you power, the power to be who you truly are. Coming more from your heart, in your responses to life, you will begin to create the quality of life experiences you really want. The real power of manifestation lies within the heart. By coming clearly in touch with the needs of your heart, what your heart wants or does not want, you are more able to manifest. Give your need out clearly to the universe and let it go, trusting that your needs will be met. You do not need to make the manifestation happen. You only need to trust. Letting-go is important as you actually prevent the manifestation from happening by not freeing the energy and allowing it to happen. This is more of a process of attunement where there is a surrender of control, a trust and an acceptance that what comes to you is in harmony with your real needs. When you attempt to manifest purely with the mind through the use of affirmation and visualization, you are making it happen. There is active mental involvement and control.

The more heart-directed your energies become, the less mind-directed you become. Your trust builds and you are able to live more and more surrendered to life itself. Through this trust and surrender, man can come closer to his spiritual dimension and begin to integrate his spirit within the heart. The heart is the gateway to the spirit. There is no detour to God.

Life is an expression of God and each individual is a unique part of that expression and is a part of God. Each person is intimately connected with God or the source and in actuality, nothing is but God. Only God is, but your ego-self separates from God simply through the creation of the "thought" of the I-self. This illusion creates the illusion of two not one, of being separate. Thus the search, the journey, the path to return to the source but even the journey is an illusion and there is no place to go. God has always been here and you have never been there or separate from God. You only think that you have been and when you come completely present, in the moment, with awareness, you will know God. Your total experience will be God.

# PART II

# CHAPTER I

# SHIFTING
CONSCIOUSNESS

Where you focus attention is where energy goes. If you focus energy on past issues or on future issues, you remove your energy from the present and live in past memories within the mind or in a projected idea of the future. In either case, your energy is diverted, from experiencing the present moment, into mental activity. You become detached from the present moment and your energy. When you become detached from your energy, your vitality and aliveness diminishes. You lose your direct experience and connection to your energy and you begin to die energetically and to become old. When the spirit is awake and pulsating within the body, filling the person with vitality, the person seems ageless. Indeed, energy is beyond time and is a function of the eternal moment. Living in the present, experiencing the current flow of universal life energy, is to experience timelessness and space-lessness. To become a pure, clear presence in the moment, is to transcend death in life and is to experience your deathlessness. To live in the past or future is to live in the dimension of time and space and is to invite senility and aging. One does not age in the eternal moment.

You have choice. At every moment of your lives, you have choice. What you choose to do with this choice can make you free. Every individual has the same ability to choose. Where you choose to focus your attention is where your energy goes. In this way, you are responsible for creating your life. You can choose to scatter your energy or to focus your energy. You can choose to live in the past, the future or the present. You can choose to think you die or to know eternalness. You have a wide range of choice and what you choose for yourselves reflects the limitations you put on yourselves or the limitations of others about life that you have accepted and come to believe as truth. The universe is an impartial supermarket, and will provide you with whatever you expect.

Each individual is unique in his personal limitations but the universe accommodates everyone. No one gets what they don't want. In shifting consciousness, it is important to recognize and accept this fact and to accept that you are not a victim. Then you can honor your choice and begin to choose to respond to life in nurturing ways.

Focusing attention and energy is, for many people, in this highly stimulated world, a major task. However, this is a significant factor towards the evolvement and expansion of consciousness. When energy is scattered in many directions, it is diffused, losing its potency and intensity. The ability to focus and direct one's energy, in the present, is a preliminary step towards shifting consciousness. Now this process will unfold naturally as you focus your attention. The more focussed and aware you become, the more obvious will be the changes. Awareness is a fire which literally burns away the debris within you, consuming and illuminating the darkness within your energy system. You are all potentially pure channels of universal life energy and need only clear your energy system and maintain this clarity to be crystal clear channels. Clearing your energy system through the fire of awareness can happen only in the present moment.

There are many focusing techniques currently practiced in the world, from ancient to contemporary traditions. The most significant factor in choosing a technique of practice is that it fit you and meet your unique needs as well as to facilitate your growth. The technique must serve you rather than you serving the technique. Technique is only a starting point and needs to evolve as you do. Try technique on to see if it fits you. You are the only one who knows what fits you and what is right for you. Nobody knows what is best for you and you must choose your way. There are many paths to help you grow and evolve consciousness but each individual will eventually begin to create his own path. This shift or movement into the conscious creation of your path happens when you can listen to your hearts, as well as your minds, and know what it is you truly want and need each moment.

# CHAPTER II

# ORGANIC KNOWING

There is a way of knowing that does not involve mind processing. While the knowing may manifest in the mind, this will come more as a spontaneous thought rather than as a conclusive thought or the product of processing many other thoughts. The mind is not involved in an analytical way but rather acts to synthesize information received from other levels of your being. This synthesis appears as a clear, direct spontaneous thought, realization or knowing.

Awareness and intellectual knowing are not synonymous yet the intellect is indirectly involved in awareness. It is because the mind is involved that people confuse intellectual knowing with knowingness. To know at purely an intellectual or mental

level is a limited way of knowing and does not en-
compass the fullness of your being. Unfortunately,
contemporary society places much value on the
mind and this creates societies where man becomes a mental genius in comparison to his development at other levels of his being. The emotional
or spiritual or physical quadrants of man may lag
far behind, creating much imbalance within the
whole society.

There are many levels of knowing. You can
know intellectually at a mental level. You can
know psychically. You can know emotionally,
through the heart as well as knowing in the body.
You can know at the cellular level. You can also
know by becoming empty and allowing knowledge
to channel through you from your spiritual quad-
rant. Each of these ways of knowing is available to
everyone and are often experienced spontaneously. In moments of knowing, you know beyond
any doubt, beyond even the ability to communi-
cate your certainty of the knowing and beyond
even how you know. You just know and your
knowingness involves much more of you than simply your mind.

All that you are and ever have been is encoded
within your cells. The cells contain a complete im-
print of your total experience. Everything that you

are is imprinted within the nucleus of the cell. As you evolve, your cells evolve and change. As your consciousness evolves, so does the consciousness of the cell and this creates a change energetically within the cell.

Change is total and is registered at all levels of your beingness. You are affected by what happens to you at all levels. Thus, change that occurs at the emotional level or at the mental level also affects you at a cellular level.

Not only does the body retain complete memory, within the cell, but it also has a deep inner sense of timing. Just as nature has a knowingness about the span and cycles of the seasons, so too does the human body innately know its own cycles and rhythms. The body goes through natural cycles, just as nature does, and is indeed in-tune with the natural timing of nature. This sense of timing comes from within the cells themselves. The body has a innate integrity and knows what it needs and when it needs it. Each body is unique and responds to its own inner clock. The body's inner sense of timing is the only true guide to knowing the cycles of individual change and movement in natural sequence. Attempting to alter or speed up the natural cycles and movements of the body is to create a premature condition which can weaken the whole structure and can create much difficulty later on. You do not alter or speed up a pregnancy. If a child is born without completing the natural pregnancy cycle, you say the child is premature. Likewise, a premature state can be created within the cells of the body if natural process is disturbed. Though there would visibly appear to be little activity during pregnancy, much subtle, vital activity is occurring. So too, do you continue to change even in times of stillness and seeming inactivity.

Man is a movement of energies which need to move in sequence and in response to natural process with integrity and harmony.

# CHAPTER III

# COMPLETING THE CIRCLE

Life is a series of many births and many deaths. The death of the physical body is only one dimension of death. There are many ways in which you die. Both death and birth can happen to you on many levels.

As you move through the cycles and seasons of growth, you are creating and evolving your soul. Life is for acquiring the building blocks of your soul, to fund the resources of your soul and to facilitate the growth of your soul toward full creative expression.

When your soul chooses to incarnate on the earth, you are also choosing to deal with issues of dualism in all its aspects. The earth is by its very nature and structure dualistic. Consequently, your life is filled with polarity such as north-south, day-night, positive-negative, man-woman, and birth-death. You move between the pillars of dualism, choosing one pillar and then the other, as you perceive the poles as separate and apart, as two. You continue to be caught up in this polarity dance until you see that the two are really one; not separate but an integral part of the whole.

The thought of separatism is what creates separatism — only a thought. With this thought, man creates much conflict, for he sees himself as separate and different from the whole. He creates himself as one pole and the rest of the world as the other pole and from this I-Thou context, man tries to relate. However, as long as man sees himself as separate from the whole, he is coming from a basic position of inner separatism and conflict rather than from a context of wholeness and harmony. Man does not see that he is the whole. Though man is never separate from the whole, he thinks he is and this illusion creates the conflict and pain of separatism. This inner conflict and duality, created and experienced by man, is reflected and manifested externally in his environment. Man is given the opportunity and choice to work with dualism in his world and in his experiences until he comes to know the one within the two and that he himself is not separate or isolated, but is one with the whole.

Your growth towards integration and wholeness is growth towards the completion of the circle. The circle ends where you began, united and merged with the whole. The circle represents wholeness, the essence of your true nature towards which you are returning.

While you are incarnated within a physical form it is important to honor and recognize the interconnection between your physical and spiritual dimensions and to not exclude either dimension or create polarization between these two dimensions by judging one above or below the other. The physical body is not the lesser vehicle. The physical body is the spiritual vehicle. The essence of spirit is contained within the physical, within form. The spirit is not separate or isolated from you and neither is heaven or hell separate from your physical life. Heaven and hell exist right here, right now within the physical world and reflect the quality and nature of your experiences which you create for yourself. As long as you remain polarized between the spiritual and physical dimensions of your being, you will remain in conflict and will relate to all outside of yourself as separate. This inner separation and conflict is the experience of hell regardless of whether you polarize with either the physical or the spiritual dimensions. Polarization of any kind represents imbalance, disintegration and separation, and is the source of conflict. Heaven and hell are inner spaces and represent the quality of your life experience. What you create as your experience in the physical form, you also create when you leave the physical world. Your consciousness continues after physical death and continues to evolve step-by-step in sequence as it did in life. You continue to create your soul through your experience and to learn the lessons you are needing to integrate as you move towards completion of the circle. The beginning and the end of the circle are one and when you come to know this oneness of spirit and form within your experience of yourselves, you will know your wholeness and will experience heaven right here, right now.

# CHAPTER IV

# CHANGING IN ORDER

The earth has consciousness and this consciousness is imprinted within every minute particle of the planet and is a record of the total history of the planet. Like your bodies, this history is registered within the cells which come together to create the earth. The consciousness of the earth is intimately linked with the consciousness of man. As mankind expands his consciousness, the vibrations of the whole planet are raised accordingly.

There is a sequencing within the universe which creates a natural ordering of events from the universal to the cellular level and without which chaos would result. All things within the universe are interdependent and inter-connected. The planet itself is in a constant state of flux but while the changes are continuous, there is a fundamental order to the change and a significance for the ordering of events. All things work together in nature and each aspect involved forms another link in the chain of events. If one of the links is missing, the whole chain is weakened and may collapse. This is a very important and significant factor for mankind to hear and to respond to NOW in the evolution of the planet. It is vital that mankind realize that natural order and balance cannot be manipulated, disturbed or altered without threatening the existence of the planet. When one element in nature is depleted or altered, this creates a chain reaction in the whole of nature which is often undetectable by man.

One of the difficulties in man's attempts to appreciate the balance and wholeness in nature is that an individual's life-span is extremely short compared to the life-span of the planet. Man experiences a narrow spectrum of time during his incarnation and cannot know the full extent of growth and evolutionary changes that have taken place within the earth to the present time and he may not live long enough to see the possible negative effects of the changes he initiated.

The earth responds to energy and the vibrations which are put into it. As the planet is a living body or organism, it will respond when the quality of energy being absorbed becomes too toxic. Then the planet will cleanse itself in whatever way is needed. The earth is a living body as is your physical body. If your physical body were exploited and filled with as many toxins as the earth is, it would not long endure. How much more exploitation can the earth body endure?

Awareness and consciousness are the most significant factors for man, at this point, in his relationship to the earth. It is essential that man act from clarity and awareness in his actions towards the earth to prevent further destruction. The imbalance within nature, on the planet, has reached devastating levels and will take the right action of many to begin to heal the earth and to reverse the present course. A major shift in consciousness in relating to the earth is needed by mankind. The earth is the body of mankind and is not separate from man. The elements which compose the earth are identical to those which compose the physical body. The earth body, like the human body, has an innate consciousness which knows when to cleanse and clear itself to regain harmony and balance. If you want to truly heal the earth, you must begin to love the earth as you would your own body. Token political gestures which appear to be relieving the destruction are not effective for the spirit from which these gestures come is greed, not a true caring and honoring of the earth. The vibrations of love are very powerful. Love is the only thing that heals. It will take much love to heal the earth. The earth knows and responds to this vibration.

The extent of man's consciousness can be measured by the quality of his relationship to the earth. When man becomes fully conscious, he will honor and embrace the earth as an integral dimension of himself, for his own physical and spiritual dimensions will then be as one and this integration will be reflected in his relationship to everything.

At this point, what can be done to heal the earth is for each individual to heal himself. Through the process of self-healing, awareness and consciousness develop which alter the quality of energy. This same principle applies whether at a cellular or global level. The healing of the earth starts with the healing of the individual.

Each individual carries within his heart the light of spirit. Though the door to the heart may be closed, just the simple awareness that the door is closed is the first step to opening the door. The individual is the only one who can access his own spirit. Guides and masters come in many forms and can help to point the way but ultimately you must find your own way.

Life is full of opportunity. The universe is constantly giving you opportunities to become aware and awake. Be grateful for what comes to you for it is an opportunity for you to awaken. When you can appreciate the gift, the blessing in disguise, you will begin to see with different eyes and hear with different ears.

# CHAPTER V

# ONWARDS

The quality and continuation of life on the planet as well as the future of the planet itself depends on the individual. It is through the individual that change must come, first, at the personal level. Only then is the individual able to be a healing influence in the world. You cannot give away what you do not have integrated within you. This is fundamental to all healing. Healing is an individual matter, a soul matter, of which only you know. Everything is to be gained through the healing process. Man will be restored to his godliness and the earth will be restored to the Garden of Eden.

*Each person has the ability to respond to himself and his life situations.*

*Each person has the capacity to heal himself and bring his energies into harmony and balance.*

*Each person has the ability to love himself with total acceptance.*

*Each person has the capacity to know and express their truth.*

*Each person has the ability to experience his own divinity.*

*Each person has the capacity to know wholeness and oneness with all.*

*Each person has the ability to know and express the essence of their heart.*

*Each person has the capacity to know the inner light of spirit.*

*Each person has the ability to sow love in all he relates to.*

*Each person has the capacity to create his own existence.*

*Each person has the ability to choose whatever he wants in life.*

*Each person has the capacity to use power creatively and constructively in their life.*

*Each person has the ability to embrace and honor the uniqueness of himself.*

*Each person has the capacity to expand consciousness to include the many ways of knowing.*

*Each person has the ability to change energy and to focus energy.*

*Each person has the capacity to increase his awareness of himself to include all his dimensions.*

*Each person has the ability to accept response-ability for his life.*

*Each person has the capacity to learn the lessons of life willingly and openly.*

*Each person has the ability to live fully and express himself fully and creatively.*

*Each person has the capacity to expand towards his potential.*